VERBAL REASONING 1
MULTIPLE CHOICE
PAPER 1

ALPHA SERIES
PRACTICE PAPERS

INSTRUCTIONS FOR PUPIL

1. You have 50 minutes to complete this test. Do not open this booklet until told to do so.

2. Do not write your answers in this booklet. Draw a line in the box thus ⊟ next to the correct answer in the answer booklet.

3. Use a pencil and if you make a mistake rub out your mark and then mark the correct box.

4. Work through the questions as quickly and as carefully as you can. Each question is worth one mark so do not spend too long on an individual question.

5. If you finish early, check your work and have another attempt at any questions you have not answered.

6. You are not allowed to ask questions during the test. If you do not understand something try your best with it then move on to the next question.

The gang use a code so that their messages cannot be understood by other people. Instead of letters, they use symbols and numbers. Work out the words using the code. Mark your answer in the answer booklet.

A	B	C	D	E	F	G	H	I	J	K	L	M
✡	✛	✜	✤	✢	◆	◇	★	☆	✪	✮	✯	✯

N	O	P	Q	R	S	T	U	V	W	X	Y	Z
✬	✫	☆	✳	✴	✶	✴	✴	✦	✷	✸	✹	✺

1. ★✤✤✳
2. ☆☆
3. ✳★✤
4. ☆★♣
5. ✛✡✳☆
6. ✡✳
7. ★☆♣★☆◇★✳
8. ✳☆✳★
9. ✸★✳✳
10. ✳☆✳✤★

A B C D E F G H I J K L M N O P Q R S T U V W X Y Z

You need to crack the following codes. Use the alphabet above to help you.

11.	If GDM means	HEN,	what does	BNKS mean?
12.	If QJMF means	PILE,	what does	NFFU mean?
13.	If 6145 means	FADE,	what does	8945 mean?
14.	If 254 means	BED,	what does	314 mean?
15.	If MKVG means	KITE,	what does	ICXG mean?
16.	If 4554 means	DEED,	what does	4935 mean?
17.	If 3175 means	CAGE,	what does	6135 mean?
18.	If NPPU means	MOOT,	what does	SPTF mean?
19.	If ILSB means	LOVE,	what does	HFPP mean?
20.	If 328 means	BAG,	what does	4286 mean?

Four children buy a bag of four different coloured sweets. There are eight sweets, two of each colour, but luckily the children like different flavours. Mary likes black but not green or blue ones, Jason likes blue but not red. Susan likes red but not black, Emma likes green but not blue.

The table below shows which other colour each child gets.

	BLACK	RED	BLUE	GREEN
Mary	✔			
Jason			✔	
Susan		✔		
Emma				✔

We have put a tick to show one colour each child gets. Mark in your answer booklet the other colour sweet each child gets.

21.	Mary
22.	Jason
23.	Susan
24.	Emma

For these next six questions find the word in the brackets which is in the same group as the two words in front of the brackets. Mark your answer in the answer booklet.

25.	Germany, Spain	(country, Europe, France, Africa, continent)
26.	pen, pencil	(ink, writing, school, crayon, book)
27.	car, lorry	(yacht, pram, bus, aeroplane, bicycle)
28.	fish, bird	(thrush, mammal, mackerel, dog, herring)
29.	window, door	(glass, wardrobe, wall, mirror, wallpaper)
30.	John, Samantha	(boy, child, Jason, name, adult)

A B C D E F G H I J K L M N O P Q R S T U V W X Y Z

For question 31 - 39 you are asked to complete the sequence for each group. You need to mark both letters in the answer booklet.

31.	C	F	I	?	?		
32.	Y	W	U	?	?		
33.	A	C	F	J	?	?	
34.	C	Z	D	Y	E	?	?
35.	M	A	N	B	?	?	P
36.	G	H	I	J	?	?	
37.	A	D	G	J	?	?	
38.	A	E	I	?	Z	V	R ?
39.	K	L	N	Q	?	?	

A B C D E F G H I J K L M N O P Q R S T U V W X Y Z

These next ten questions require you to arrange the words alphabetically then find the word which is third alphabetically. Mark your answer in the answer booklet.

40.	wonder	wander	wearily	warship	wiggle
41.	jumper	justice	joyful	juncture	jamboree
42.	running	retrace	rustic	restore	repress
43.	hitting	happen	helpless	heavily	hearty
44.	relation	reader	riddle	rocky	relegate
45.	puncture	peaceful	princess	predator	pedantic
46.	anxious	armistice	access	anorak	ambition
47.	slowly	sorrowful	suture	sorcerer	space
48.	plastic	palace	poultice	precursor	prelate
49.	laugh	leader	licence	lively	livery

The words in each of the groups below have something in common with each other and nothing in common with the words in the other groups. For each question find the letter of the group you think the word belongs in.

A	**B**	**C**	**D**	**E**
large	car	igloo	tiger	daffodil
massive	van	tent	cheetah	rose
enormous	lorry	wigwam	giraffe	daisy

Example: Truck is (**B**) because a truck, like the words in Group B, is a form of transport.

50.	hut
51.	leopard
52.	motorbike
53.	gladioli
54.	huge
55.	tulip
56.	gigantic
57.	shack

For the next set of questions you need to do some more code cracking, however this time numbers are used instead of symbols. To help you the word CROP is represented by the numerals 6712. Work out the set of numerals which represent each of the other two words and use the code to find the other words represented by the numerals in questions 58-65.

6712	2135	5364	⇨	CROP	TUCK	POUT

58.	7115
59.	6115
60.	2712
61.	57364
62.	57135
63.	6375
64.	7135
65.	2174

Find the odd-word-out from each list. An example is given to help you. Mark your answer in the answer booklet.

	toffee	chocolate	caramel	sherbert	cheese
66.	piano	catapult	flute	violin	harp
67.	curry	chips	steak	omelette	ice-cream
68.	sketch	picture	painting	glass	drawing
69.	ruby	sapphire	necklace	emerald	diamond
70.	wood	cotton	silk	wool	linen
71.	Britain	Albania	Argentina	Australia	Africa
72.	broccoli	carrot	marrow	turnip	apple
73.	cat	monkey	fish	dog	cow
74.	bush	oak	elm	beech	sycamore
75.	bicycle	boat	car	bus	motorbike

These questions require you to consider the relationship between words. Find the word from each pair of brackets which is similar in its relationship to the word in front of the brackets. You need to mark <u>two</u> words in your answer booklet, one from each pair of brackets.

76. | Four is to (eight, figure, book) as Two is to (number, four, maths).

77. | Wool is to (cat, cow, sheep) as Silk is to (garden, worm, path).

78. | Video is to (cook, read, watch) as Music is to (listen, breathe, work).

79. | Miaow is to (dog, wolf, cat) as Quack is to (goose, duck, pigeon).

80. | Snake is to (lizard, reptile, bird) as Lion is to (jungle, mammal, zoo).

81. | House is to (bricks, slate, palace) as Igloo is to (ice, shelter, cold).

82. | Train is to (ticket, seat, rails) as Van is to (noise, road, wheels).

83. | Colt is to (horse, car, fur) as Heifer is to (farm, cow, meat).

84. | Pork is to (cow, dog, pig) as Mutton is to (sheep, horse, goat).

85. | Hearing is to (head, ears, eyes) as Taste is to (tongue, nose, skin).

END OF THE TEST
Use the time remaining to retry any questions you failed to answer
and check your work.

Published by:
R & S Educational Services • 23 Manor Square • Otley • West Yorkshire • LS21 3AP
Printed by - Chippendale Press • 65 Bondgate • Otley • West Yorkshire • LS21 3AB

VERBAL REASONING 1
MULTIPLE CHOICE
PAPER 2

ALPHA SERIES
PRACTICE PAPERS

INSTRUCTIONS FOR PUPIL

1. You have 50 minutes to complete this test. Do not open this booklet until told to do so.

2. Do not write your answers in this booklet. Draw a line in the box thus ▭ next to the correct answer in the answer booklet.

3. Use a pencil and if you make a mistake rub out your mark and then mark the correct box.

4. Work through the questions as quickly and as carefully as you can. Each question is worth one mark so do not spend too long on an individual question.

5. If you finish early, check your work and have another attempt at any questions you have not answered.

6. You are not allowed to ask questions during the test. If you do not understand something try your best with it then move on to the next question.

In this set of questions, find the odd-word-out from each list. Mark your answer in the answer booklet.

1.	quaver	crotchet	minim	breve	music
2.	tent	igloo	garage	house	cottage
3.	witch	elf	fairy	tale	goblin
4.	Mars	Saturn	Earth	Moon	Uranus
5.	snow	salt	rice	black	flour
6.	London	city	town	hamlet	village
7.	aspirin	lozenge	pill	swallow	tablet
8.	television	view	radio	theatre	cinema
9.	mint	parsley	grass	oregano	thyme
10.	chair	table	settee	sofa	bench

A B C D E F G H I J K L M N O P Q R S T U V W X Y Z

You are asked here to complete the sequence. For these questions, the letters are in pairs. The alphabet will help you to answer the questions.

11.	ZA	YB	XC	WD	?
12.	AZ	CW	ET	GQ	?
13.	ML	?	MJ	MI	MH
14.	QN	AC	NK	CE	?
15.	BA	ZY	DC	XW	?
16.	AE	EI	IM	?	
17.	ZY	YW	WT	?	

18. Ray has more pocket money than Terry but less than Ernest and Andrew. Andrew has less than Mark. Terry receives less than Ray but more than Steven. How many people get less pocket money than Ray?

19. King Arthur reigned for longer than King Richard but less than King Charles. King Charles reigned for fewer years than King Henry and King James. Whose reign was the shortest?

20. Five dogs were taken for a walk by their owners. Rover's walk lasted for longer than that of Breaks and Joey but less than that of Bristle. Max walked for longer than Breaks and less than Joey. Which dog had the shortest walk?

This set of questions requires you to form two new words by moving one letter from the first word in capitals and placing it anywhere in the second word in capitals so that two new words are formed. An example is given to help you. Mark your answer in the answer booklet.

EXAMPLE:

ACHE and WAS make <u>ACE</u> *and* <u>WASH</u> *because the H is moved from the first word to the second.*

21. RAID and ICE make ? and ?

22. CLOUD and ARE make ? and ?

23. WASP and SEER make ? and ?

24. PAINT and SAD make ? and ?

25. STAND and ILL make ? and ?

26. TEAR and OVER make ? and ?

27. WEAR and DAM make ? and ?

In a car race, there are four teams: Vauxwagon, Citrat, Datsari and Fiazda. Each team competes once with each of the other three. The Vauxwagon team loses to the Citrat team but beats the Datsari team which loses to the Fiazda team. The Fiazda team beats the Vauxwagon team but loses to the Citrat team which beats the Datsari team.

28. | How many races does the Vauxwagon team win?

29. | How many races does the Fiazda team win?

30. | How many races does the Citrat team win?

31. | How many races does the Datsari team win?

A B C D E F G H I J K L M N O P Q R S T U V W X Y Z

For the following questions work out the relationship between the first two sets of letters or numbers to solve the question. Use the alphabet above to help you.

32. | If BKHLA means CLIMB, what does SVHBD mean?

33. | If OSGAI means QUICK, what does QJMU mean?

34. | If 133545 means ACCEDE, what does 4516 mean?

35. | If EQRG means COPE, what does VCRG mean?

36. | If 497 means DIG, what does 2556 mean?

37. | If 935 means ICE, what does 6135 mean?

38. | If 25138 means BEACH, what does 25538 mean?

39. | If 1385 means ACHE, what does 1754 mean?

40. | If 4516 means DEAF, what does 38945 mean?

41. | If 11, 2, 20, 16, 15 means JASON, what does 11, 2, 15, 6 mean?

For the following questions you are required to crack the code. You need to find out which symbol stands for each letter and then identify the coded words. Mark your answer in the answer booklet.

FEET	FETE	LEVEL	FLEET	FEEL	FELT

42. ❄❄●▼

43. ●❄❖❄●

44. ❄❄❄●

45. ❄❄❄▼

46. ❄●❄❄▼

47. ❄❄▼❄

For these questions you will need to find the one word from the five words in the brackets which can be spelt using letters only from the word written in capitals.

48. ELECTRICITY (recite   tricky   lecture   cities   tracer)

49. INFILTRATE (travel   latrine   traitor   retrace   invent)

50. BOUNTIFUL (fount   full   bounty   spider   train)

51. LITIGATION (gliding   tight   nation   tonal   laugh)

52. RETROSPECT (rested   trees   return   retrace   inspect)

53. LOCOMOTIVE (moment   cockle   calmer   voted   comet)

54. SOMERSAULT (trowel   salted   moult   assemble   mercy)

55. PARTICULAR (particle   crate   trace   trail   alert)

56. INQUISITION (quaint   quite   quips   quest   quoit)

57. OSCILLOSCOPE (scintillate   loser   clasp   close   scupper)

This next set of questions asks you to put one word from the first group in front of one word from the second group to make a proper word.

EXAMPLE:

| | *break/care/run* | *up/fast/down* | = | *breakfast* |

58.	pat/go/hit	rat/share/tern
59.	pear/post/peat	age/arm/every
60.	under/between/on	hedge/ground/earth
61.	before/every/over	scales/weight/height
62.	up/down/in	sell/buy/keep
63.	wake/care/take	even/less/more
64.	my/at/be	man/self/person
65.	before/now/after	soon/noon/late
66.	drag/pull/heave	off/it/on
67.	pig/horse/cow	mud/sticky/pat

Find the two words, one from each list, which are similar in meaning.

EXAMPLE:

| | *pupil, lesson, book* | *student, desk, chalk* |

68.	small, mouse, big	bit, piece, little
69.	quick, quiet, queer	quaint, fast, slow
70.	stare, smile, look	face, chin, grin
71.	go, run, walk	stroll, roll, fall
72.	where, wonder, wander	question, answer, request
73.	success, access, excess	entrance, exit, cinema
74.	gentle, justice, peace	soft, blonde, lore
75.	greasy, spots, bits	acne, arms, legs
76.	clear, water, seaside	nice, good, pure
77.	socks, laundry, money	washing, dishes, kitchen

Find the word which would appear fourth in each list when arranged alphabetically.

EXAMPLE:

| felled | furious | future | friendship | _furore_ |

The answer is furore because the alphabetical order is:

1. felled
2. friendship
3. furious
4. furore
5. future

78.	bough	bottle	battle	brainless	billowed
79.	tracking	though	through	trodden	tickle
80.	deaden	doctor	dreamed	duchess	delicious
81.	marquis	mistress	monstrous	monastic	manners
82.	nettle	noiseless	neither	neighbour	negligence
83.	orator	outface	opened	oppress	occasion
84.	unlace	useless	usually	umpire	urchin
85.	closed	called	cleverly	compress	crater

END OF THE TEST
Use the time remaining to retry any questions you failed to answer
and check your work.

© R & S EDUCATIONAL SERVICES
Alpha Series 1993
Verbal Reasoning - Multiple Choice 2000

Published by:
R & S Educational Services • 23 Manor Square • Otley • West Yorkshire • LS21 3AP
Printed by - Chippendale Press • 65 Bondgate • Otley • West Yorkshire • LS21 3AB

VERBAL REASONING 1
MULTIPLE CHOICE
PAPER 3

ALPHA SERIES
PRACTICE PAPERS

INSTRUCTIONS FOR PUPIL

1. You have 50 minutes to complete this test. Do not open this booklet until told to do so.

2. Do not write your answers in this booklet. Draw a line in the box thus ▭ next to the correct answer in the answer booklet.

3. Use a pencil and if you make a mistake rub out your mark and then mark the correct box.

4. Work through the questions as quickly and as carefully as you can. Each question is worth one mark so do not spend too long on an individual question.

5. If you finish early, check your work and have another attempt at any questions you have not answered.

6. You are not allowed to ask questions during the test. If you do not understand something try your best with it then move on to the next question.

For the following questions, select the one statement which must be true from the information given. Mark your answer in the answer booklet.

1. **Coffee is a drink and no drinks are solid.**

   a. Coffee is a powder.

   b. Coffee is a liquid.

   c. Coffee is not a solid.

   d. Coffee can be drunk with or without milk.

2. **Trees have leaves and no animals have leaves.**

   a. Animals are trees without leaves.

   b. Trees have leaves in summer.

   c. Animals are green.

   d. Trees are not animals.

3. **The heart is a kind of organ and organs are not musical.**

   a. The heart pumps the blood.

   b. The heart lies inside the breast.

   c. The heart is not a musical instrument.

   d. People don't have hearts.

4. **Wheat is a type of cereal and no cereals are vegetables.**

   a. Bread is made from wheat.

   b. Wheat is not a vegetable.

   c. Wheat is harvested in Spring.

   d. Wheat is a weed.

5. **Egypt is in Africa and Africa lies south of Europe.**

   a. Egypt lies on the Mediterranean.

   b. Egypt is smaller than Wales.

   c. Europe is north of Egypt.

   d. Egypt contains pyramids.

Shops A & B sell newspapers and milk. Shops C & D sell sweets and stationery. Shops A & D sell milk and sweets.

6. | Which shop sells both newspapers and sweets?

7. | Which shop sells both milk and stationery?

---

8. | Julie is older than Ken but younger than Tom and Jerry. Tom is younger than Jerry. Who was born last?

9. | Istia lies to the west of Damatia and east of Riskland. Grestoland is east of Damatia and west of Estinia. Travelling westwards from Grestoland which would be the first country you would pass through?

10. | Jeff and Sally like riding motorbikes. Sally and Kim like riding bicycles. Kim and Jeff like riding horses. Who enjoys riding both motorbikes and horses?

Select two words, one from each list, which are similar in meaning. Mark <u>both</u> words in the answer booklet.

11.	inquire	invest	interest		ask	tell	reveal
12.	convex	perspex	perplex		game	jigsaw	puzzle
13.	retrieve	rest	reprieve		carry	fetch	buy
14.	fun	happiness	sadness		outside	sorrow	tears
15.	mend	expensive	exchange		market	buy	transfer
16.	peak	look	hear		same	summit	some
17.	to	two	too		less	also	only
18.	carefully	speedily	slowly		truly	gently	quickly
19.	diamond	sparkle	ruby		glitter	emerald	sapphire

You need to consider the relationship between words. For this group of ten questions find two words, one from each set of brackets, which are similar in their relationship to the words in front of the brackets. Mark **both** words in the answer booklet.

20. Piano is to (music, notes, keyboard) as Violin is to (songs, strings, sound).

21. Radio is to (programme, screen, sound) as Television is to (seats, sight, play).

22. Tapestry is to (wool, needle, old) as Picture is to (drawing, paintbrush, sketch).

23. Tragedy is to (ending, theatre, sad) as Comedy is to (funny, clown, new).

24. One is to (one, two, three) as Two is to (four, five, double).

25. Terror is to (danger, fear, trouble) as Sorrow is to (sadness, feeling, emotion).

26. Snow is to (rain, wind, flakes) as hail is to (wet, stones, winter).

27. Jet is to (trail, roar, speed) as Car is to (exhaust, noise, fumes).

28. Pork is to (fry, pig, grill) as Mutton is to (sheep, farm, wool).

29. Rug is to (carpet, floor, furry) as Wallpaper is to (wall, floral, stripes).

A B C D E F G H I J K L M N O P Q R S T U V W X Y Z

Use the alphabet to help you solve the codes. Mark your answer in the answer booklet.

30. If FQDDM = GREEN then AKTD = ?

31. If EMJB = GOLD then KGLC = ?

32. If EFTL = DESK then SPPN = ?

33. If TCKP = RAIN then UWP = ?

34. If TKM = WIN then LTA = ?

35. If IDFH = FACE then QRVH = ?

36. If EFAB = HIDE then PBBH = ?

37. If UECP = SCAN then TKO = ?

38. If VDLO = SAIL then ZHW = ?

PAGE 3

This set of questions requires you to find the odd-word-out. Mark your answer in the answer booklet.

39.	franc, peseta, pasta, cent, penny
40.	picnic, banquet, meal, starvation, buffet
41.	soap, toothpaste, flannel, fork, bubblebath
42.	carrot, pork, beef, chicken, lamb
43.	grumpy, grizzle, moping, grand, moaning
44.	satin, silk, cotton, wool, crimplene
45.	port, wine, coffee, brandy, champagne
46.	brass, gold, silver, emerald, diamond
47.	plaice, pike, cod, haddock, sole
48.	fantasy, pleurisy, pneumonia, bronchitis, asthma

Place one word from the first group in front of one word from the second group to make a new real word. Mark your answer in the answer booklet.

49.	pub / in / inn	quick / quest / quiet
50.	for / four / flaw	ten / tiny / teen
51.	bill / bob / frank	invite / incense / incur
52.	child / children / school	nuts / hood / wood
53.	goat / farm / kid	near / not / nap
54.	clever / cope / manage	good / quiet / able
55.	pair / part / past	ridge / hill / top
56.	queer / quest / quiet	ion / any / on
57.	how / nobody / every	which / where / what

For the next nine questions you will need to use the table below. This table shows the price per pound of five vegetables throughout the different seasons of the year. Find the information from the table for the following questions.

	Winter	Spring	Summer	Autumn
Carrots	22p	39p	37p	69p
Leeks	30p	60p	75p	56p
Cabbage	90p	75p	35p	70p
Sprouts	25p	40p	46p	61p
Cauliflower	30p	64p	93p	42p

58.   In which season are carrots more expensive than cabbages?

59.   Which is the most expensive vegetable in Autumn?

60.   In which season are sprouts more expensive than cabbages?

61.   Which is the cheapest vegetable in Autumn?

62.   In which season are two vegetables the same price?

63.   In which season are sprouts more expensive than leeks?

64.   In which season are sprouts cheaper than carrots?

65.   What is the most expensive season to buy leeks?

66.   Which vegetable is the cheapest to buy in winter?

In a soccer competition there are 5 teams, A, B, C, D and E. B loses to A and D but beats C. D beats C. A wins over C and E but loses to D. E beats B and C then loses to D.

67.   How many games does A win?

68.   How many games does B lose?

69.   How many games does C win?

70.   How many games does D lose?

71.   How many games does E win?

72.   Which team finished second?

Find three words, one word from each pair of brackets, in order to make the most logical sentence.

73. | The (cow, horse, kangaroo) was seen (bucking, moaning, driving) on the (colourful, crazy, windy) day.

74. | (Flowers, computers, records) were (invented, revolved, picked) in the (fields, hotel, desk).

75. | How many (pennies, pounds, cents) are there in the (Japanese, Italian, American) (lire, yen, dollar).

76. | The (ant, duck, buffalo) was (blown, run, washed) away by (frozen, running, sticky) water poured on its nest.

77. | She wore (jodhpurs, skates, skis) to go (running, riding, racing) her (lake, horse, windmill).

78. | The (man, judge, drunkard) drank (alcohol, quickly, water) and spent the night on a (bench, tree, school) in the park.

79. | She sent a (packet, postcard, pen) from her (prison, holiday, chateau) in (Torquay, torment, terror).

80. | (Pepper, vinegar, salt) was used to (poison, cover, flavour) the (grass, potatoes, steam) as they boiled.

81. | The (blind, actresses, spiders) use (vibrations, touch, sight) to (explore, invent, destroy) the world.

Alex speaks Russian and French. Jan speaks Dutch and Spanish. Ivan speaks Russian and Arabic. Rebecca speaks Arabic and Greek. Gwen speaks Russian and French.

82. | Who would not be able to speak to any of the others if they were sitting together in a room?

83. | How many would be able to communicate with more than one other person in the room?

84. | Which language can the majority of the people speak?

85. | To how many people can Gwen speak?

END OF THE TEST
Use the time remaining to retry any questions you failed to answer
and check your work.

Published by:
R & S Educational Services • 23 Manor Square • Otley • West Yorkshire • LS21 3AP
Printed by - Chippendale Press • 65 Bondgate • Otley • West Yorkshire • LS21 3AB

VERBAL REASONING 1
MULTIPLE CHOICE
PAPER 4

ALPHA SERIES
PRACTICE PAPERS

INSTRUCTIONS FOR PUPIL

1. You have 50 minutes to complete this test. Do not open this booklet until told to do so.

2. Do not write your answers in this booklet. Draw a line in the box thus ▭ next to the correct answer in the answer booklet.

3. Use a pencil and if you make a mistake rub out your mark and then mark the correct box.

4. Work through the questions as quickly and as carefully as you can. Each question is worth one mark so do not spend too long on an individual question.

5. If you finish early, check your work and have another attempt at any questions you have not answered.

6. You are not allowed to ask questions during the test. If you do not understand something try your best with it then move on to the next question.

The table below shows the average temperature in °C at five different places during four months of the year. Answer the following questions using this information. Mark your answer in the answer booklet.

	December	April	July	September
Osterdam	-4	12	20	15
Sydbourne	31	25	10	18
Hudderspool	2	11	22	12
Croscow	-14	0	30	5
Delfi	25	30	35	20

1. | In which month does Croscow have a higher average temperature than Sydbourne?

2. | Which city has the lowest December temperature?

3. | Which city has a higher September temperature than Sydbourne?

4. | In which month does Sydbourne have a higher temperature than Delfi?

5. | Which city has the lowest April temperature?

6. | In how many cities is July the hottest month?

7. | In which month does Hudderspool have a lower temperature than Croscow?

8. | In which month does Osterdam have a lower temperature than Croscow?

9. | Which city has a higher average temperature in April than in July?

10. | Which city has the third highest temperature in December?

In the following lists one word is different to the other four words. In your answer booklet, mark the word which is the odd one out.

11.	listen	dream	hear	watch	concentrate
12.	justice	peace	government	equality	truth
13.	river	stream	estuary	tributary	island
14.	fall	mountain	glacier	summit	rock
15.	book	magazine	television	leaflet	booklet
16.	wood	paper	coal	plastic	peat
17.	star	meteor	astronaut	comet	planet
18.	necklace	gold	silver	platinum	steel

Find the one letter which will finish the first word and start the second word for both pairs of words. The letter must be the same for both pairs of words. An example is given.

WRIS (?) OW   DEN (?) IE

The answer is ' T '   (WRIS**T**, **T**OW, DEN**T**, **T**IE)

19.	CO	?	RIST		KNE	?	ENT
20.	LES	?	EEN		TOS	?	AY
21.	AN	?	EN		EN	?	OG
22.	TO	?	X		BO	?	FF
23.	CAS	?	ATE		BOT	?	EAR
24.	OA	?	EN		OU	?	USK
25.	RU	?	AT		CLU	?	INS
26.	AN	?	OG		BOL	?	ESK
27.	IN	?	ITE		LUC	?	ERB

A B C D E F G H I J K L M N O P Q R S T U V W X Y Z

The two question marks in each question represent missing letters or numbers, replace the question marks to complete the sequence for each group. Mark the <u>two</u> missing numbers or letters in your answer booklet

28.	Z	Y	W	T	?	?		
29.	D	G	E	H	F	I	?	?
30.	L	Z	O	Y	R	X	?	?
31.	T	R	P	N	?	?		
32.	1	4	7	?	?	16		
33.	0	6	0	8	0	?	?	12
34.	100	75	?	?	0			
35.	-3	3	9	?	?	27		
36.	5	6	8	?	?	20		
37.	30	27	24	?	?	15		
38.	2	4	8	?	?	64		

Find the one word from the five words in the brackets which may be spelt using only letters from the word written in capitals. Mark your answer in the answer booklet.

39. | BLANCMANGE (anchor ranch bleach manage mangy)

40. | ANNIHILATE (hinted shine thane later night)

41. | CARICATURED (rickety character traitor creature cured)

42. | GLORIFICATION (failing feeling gloried carafe glorious)

43. | DANGEROUSLY (dearest slowly wronged drowsy grouse)

44. | XYLOPHONE (phonic loop lonely helped honed)

45. | WHORTLEBERRY (horse rattle whine bother white)

46. | VOCIFERATE (rough ferry trifle every fierce)

47. | ULTRASTRUCTURE (tractor strait truth rupture state)

48. | TETRAHEDRON (their thread wrath trees drape)

For the following questions find the one statement which must be true from the information given. Mark your answer in the answer booklet.

49. | The earth is a planet and no planets are stars.

    a.   The earth is larger than the moon.

    b.   The earth revolves around the sun.

    c.   The earth is not a star.

    d.   The earth is a small star.

50. | The Thames is a river and no river flows uphill.

    a.   All rivers run to the sea.

    b.   The Thames runs through London.

    c.   The Thames does not flow uphill.

    d.   The Thames flows uphill.

Tom, Dick, Harriet and Elsa are four chess players. Each plays the others once.
Harriet beats Tom but loses against Dick and Elsa, Dick loses against Elsa but wins
over Tom. Tom loses against Elsa.

51. | How many games does Tom lose?

52. | How many games does Dick lose?

53. | How many games does Harriet lose?

54. | How many games does Elsa lose?

55. | Which player comes second?

Find the word from each pair of brackets which is similar in its relationship to the
word in front of the brackets. You need to mark <u>two</u> words in your answer booklet,
one from each pair of brackets.

56. | Bob is to (Richard, James, Robert) as Gill is to (Joan, Gillian, Jessica).

57. | Inch is to (toes, squeeze, foot) as Ounce is to (dance, pound, money).

58. | Petal is to (name, flower, grow) as Leaf is to (tree, garden, path).

59. | Zero is to (one, none, gone) as One is to (some, to, two).

60. | Catch is to (trap, catched, caught) as Buy is to (brought, shop, bought).

61. | Skin is to (pale, people, human) as Fur is to (animal, coat, hairy).

62. | Glass is to (window, break, clear) as Wood is to (hard, door, brown).

63. | Friend is to (Jenny, kind, smile) as Enemy is to (gun, mean, war).

64. | Hat is to (buy, wear, head) as Mitten is to (hand, warm, leather).

65. | On is to (one, switch, off) as In is to (out, put, go).

66. | Boots are to (leather, heels, winter) as Sandals are to (slim, summer, thin).

67. | Justice is to (fairness, courts, lawyers) as Liberty is to (statue, love, freedom).

Find the two words, one from each list, which are similar in meaning. You need to mark <u>both</u> words in your answer booklet

68.	foolish	clever	wise	silly	steady	numb
69.	weird	bad	sad	right	good	rotten
70.	politician	Labour	Tory	govern	statesman	justice
71.	fight	trite	three	stale	bread	air
72.	sage	wage	rage	fury	worry	sorry
73.	eating	drinking	food	question	hunger	chewing
74.	report	support	deport	detain	sustain	refrain
75.	handle	bangle	reveal	hold	gold	resolve
76.	new	history	old	gold	antique	shop
77.	new	yesterday	tomorrow	news	recent	modern

Instead of letters, numbers are used to spell GAME, SOON, and MIST. The three sets of numbers are 8776, 3152 and 5489. Work out which set of numbers stands for each word and use the code to find which word each group of numbers stand for.

78.	5288
79.	5779
80.	8763
81.	9452
82.	8913
83.	6289
84.	8215
85.	8463

END OF THE TEST
Use the time remaining to retry any questions you failed to answer
and check your work.

Published by:
R & S Educational Services • 23 Manor Square • Otley • West Yorkshire • LS21 3AP
Printed by - Chippendale Press • 65 Bondgate • Otley • West Yorkshire • LS21 3AB

VERBAL REASONING 1
ANSWER BOOKLET

ALPHA SERIES
PRACTICE PAPERS

GUIDANCE FOR PARENTS

The Alpha series is intended to provide children with the opportunity to become familiar with working on a range of examination papers. The style and content of the papers are appropriate for children in Years 6 and 7, i.e 10-12 years old. The papers are valuable aids for children who are due to sit examinations such as the 11+ and 12+.

Administering the Papers

It is important to select an appropriate time to give the test to your child. Choose an area which is well-lit, quiet and provide a table or desk for your child to work at.

The tests need to be timed. The actual examinations are of 50 minute duration and these Practice Papers have been devised to last the same amount of time. Please note that the examination time begins after the instructions have been read and understood.

Should you find that the recommended times are inappropriate for your child, they should be adjusted as appropriate. However the revised times should be adhered to for your child to gain experience of working under time pressure. It is useful if you can tell your child how much time is remaining at regular intervals and even more so for your child to learn to monitor the time for themselves. It is advised that you allow a gap of 2-3 days between each Paper.

Overall, the Practice Papers will be of most use where they are administered as closely to the actual examination conditions as possible.

Multiple-Choice Tests

This Alpha Series Pack contains multiple-choice type questions and the following should be observed.

Your child will need to enter his/her answers in the booklet and not on the test Papers themselves. A line should be drawn in the appropriate box thus ▭ using a pencil and any mistakes should be erased before the correct box is selected. This is important as in the actual test, answers are scanned by a computer and a line left in an incorrect box will be marked as a wrong answer. There is obviously extra scope for errors as the child has to read the question sheet and the answer booklet simultaneously. He/she should be warned of this danger and encouraged to take particular care.

Finally, a raw score should be taken. Unfortunately, it is impossible to state what is a pass mark as a set number of children will be deemed to have passed the examination each year. Accordingly, the actual pass score will vary. Please note that some questions require two or more answers. Your child must get all parts correct in such cases as no half marks are awarded.

1
- teem ☐
- loom ☐
- meet ☐
- moot ☐

2
- of ☐
- at ☐
- in ☐
- on ☐

3
- tie ☐
- sue ☐
- she ☐
- the ☐

4
- old ☐
- sky ☐
- ski ☐
- oil ☐

5
- bare ☐
- bran ☐
- barn ☐
- born ☐

6
- an ☐
- by ☐
- at ☐
- be ☐

7
- minstrel ☐
- kindling ☐
- middling ☐
- midnight ☐

8
- wind ☐
- wick ☐
- with ☐
- wish ☐

9
- yelp ☐
- your ☐
- yale ☐
- yoke ☐

10
- touch ☐
- north ☐
- torch ☐
- teach ☐

11
- coat ☐
- colt ☐
- celt ☐
- bolt ☐

12
- moon ☐
- moot ☐
- meet ☐
- heed ☐

13
- hire ☐
- hail ☐
- kind ☐
- hide ☐

14
- bad ☐
- cod ☐
- cad ☐
- cab ☐

15
- give ☐
- gave ☐
- jail ☐
- have ☐

16
- dice ☐
- dole ☐
- dime ☐
- dome ☐

17
- deaf ☐
- edge ☐
- face ☐
- fade ☐

18
- tune ☐
- rose ☐
- rope ☐
- ripe ☐

19
- lass ☐
- kill ☐
- loss ☐
- kiss ☐

20
- ache ☐
- each ☐
- cage ☐
- deaf ☐

21
- black ☐
- red ☐
- blue ☐
- green ☐

22
- black ☐
- red ☐
- blue ☐
- green ☐

23
- black ☐
- red ☐
- blue ☐
- green ☐

24
- black ☐
- red ☐
- blue ☐
- green ☐

25
- country ☐
- Europe ☐
- France ☐
- Africa ☐
- Continent ☐

26
- ink ☐
- writing ☐
- school ☐
- crayon ☐
- book ☐

27
- yacht ☐
- pram ☐
- bus ☐
- aeroplane ☐
- bicycle ☐

28
- thrush ☐
- mammal ☐
- mackerel ☐
- dog ☐
- herring ☐

29
- glass ☐
- wardrobe ☐
- wall ☐
- mirror ☐
- wallpaper ☐

30
- boy ☐
- child ☐
- Jason ☐
- name ☐
- adult ☐

31
- N ☐
- L ☐
- M ☐
- O ☐
- P ☐

32
- Q ☐
- R ☐
- S ☐
- T ☐
- U ☐

33
- L ☐
- O ☐
- P ☐
- T ☐
- U ☐

34
- F ☐
- G ☐
- Y ☐
- X ☐
- Z ☐

35
- D ☐
- Q ☐
- O ☐
- P ☐
- C ☐

36
- M ☐
- K ☐
- N ☐
- L ☐
- O ☐

37
- M ☐
- N ☐
- P ☐
- O ☐
- R ☐

38
- A ☐
- M ☐
- N ☐
- O ☐
- S ☐

39
- Z ☐
- V ☐
- T ☐
- W ☐
- U ☐

40
- wonder ☐
- wander ☐
- wearily ☐
- warship ☐
- wiggle ☐

41
- jumper ☐
- justice ☐
- joyful ☐
- juncture ☐
- jamboree ☐

42
- running ☐
- retrace ☐
- rustic ☐
- restore ☐
- repress ☐

43
- hitting ☐
- happen ☐
- helpless ☐
- heavily ☐
- hearty ☐

44
- relation ☐
- reader ☐
- riddle ☐
- rocky ☐
- relegate ☐

45
- puncture ☐
- peaceful ☐
- princess ☐
- predator ☐
- pedantic ☐

46
- anxious ☐
- armistice ☐
- access ☐
- anorak ☐
- ambition ☐

47
- slowly ☐
- sorrowful ☐
- suture ☐
- sorcerer ☐
- space ☐

48
- plastic ☐
- palace ☐
- poultice ☐
- precursor ☐
- prelate ☐

49
- laugh ☐
- leader ☐
- licence ☐
- lively ☐
- livery ☐

50
- A ☐
- B ☐
- C ☐
- D ☐
- E ☐

51
- A ☐
- B ☐
- C ☐
- D ☐
- E ☐

52
- A ☐
- B ☐
- C ☐
- D ☐
- E ☐

53
- A ☐
- B ☐
- C ☐
- D ☐
- E ☐

54
- A ☐
- B ☐
- C ☐
- D ☐
- E ☐

55
- A ☐
- B ☐
- C ☐
- D ☐
- E ☐

56
- A ☐
- B ☐
- C ☐
- D ☐
- E ☐

57
- A ☐
- B ☐
- C ☐
- D ☐
- E ☐

58
- peer ☐
- poor ☐
- root ☐
- coot ☐

59
- root ☐
- coop ☐
- coot ☐
- rout ☐

60
- port ☐
- trot ☐
- pour ☐
- prop ☐

61
- truck ☐
- crick ☐
- crock ☐
- trout ☐

62
- crick ☐
- truck ☐
- trout ☐
- crock ☐

63
- coup ☐
- cock ☐
- crop ☐
- curt ☐

64
- tour ☐
- rout ☐
- rock ☐
- ruck ☐

65
- pork ☐
- puck ☐
- port ☐
- pour ☐

EXAMPLE
- toffee ☐
- chocolate ☐
- caramel ☐
- sherbert ☐
- cheese �

66
- piano ☐
- catapult ☐
- flute ☐
- violin ☐
- harp ☐

67
- curry ☐
- chips ☐
- steak ☐
- omelette ☐
- ice-cream ☐

68
- sketch ☐
- picture ☐
- painting ☐
- glass ☐
- drawing ☐

69
- ruby ☐
- sapphire ☐
- necklace ☐
- emerald ☐
- diamond ☐

70
- wood ☐
- cotton ☐
- silk ☐
- wool ☐
- linen ☐

71
- Britain ☐
- Albania ☐
- Argentina ☐
- America ☐
- Africa ☐

72
- broccoli ☐
- carrot ☐
- marrow ☐
- turnip ☐
- apple ☐

73
- cat ☐
- monkey ☐
- fish ☐
- dog ☐
- cow ☐

74
- bush ☐
- oak ☐
- elm ☐
- beech ☐
- sycamore ☐

75
- bicycle ☐
- boat ☐
- car ☐
- bus ☐
- motorbike ☐

76
- eight ☐
- figure ☐
- book ☐
- number ☐
- four ☐
- maths ☐

77
- cat ☐
- cow ☐
- sheep ☐
- garden ☐
- worm ☐
- path ☐

78
- cook ☐
- read ☐
- watch ☐
- listen ☐
- breathe ☐
- work ☐

79
- dog ☐
- wolf ☐
- cat ☐
- goose ☐
- duck ☐
- pigeon ☐

80
- lizard ☐
- reptile ☐
- bird ☐
- jungle ☐
- mammal ☐
- zoo ☐

81
- bricks ☐
- slate ☐
- palace ☐
- ice ☐
- shelter ☐
- cold ☐

82
- ticket ☐
- seat ☐
- rails ☐
- noise ☐
- road ☐
- wheels ☐

83
- horse ☐
- car ☐
- fur ☐
- farm ☐
- cow ☐
- meat ☐

84
- cow ☐
- dog ☐
- pig ☐
- sheep ☐
- horse ☐
- goat ☐

85
- head ☐
- ears ☐
- eyes ☐
- tongue ☐
- nose ☐
- skin ☐

END OF PAPER 1

1
- quaver ☐
- crotchet ☐
- minim ☐
- breve ☐
- music ☐

2
- tent ☐
- igloo ☐
- garage ☐
- house ☐
- cottage ☐

3
- witch ☐
- elf ☐
- fairy ☐
- tale ☐
- goblin ☐

4
- Mars ☐
- Saturn ☐
- Earth ☐
- Moon ☐
- Uranus ☐

5
- snow ☐
- salt ☐
- rice ☐
- black ☐
- flour ☐

6
- London ☐
- city ☐
- town ☐
- hamlet ☐
- village ☐

7
- aspirin ☐
- lozenge ☐
- pill ☐
- swallow ☐
- tablet ☐

8
- television ☐
- view ☐
- radio ☐
- theatre ☐
- cinema ☐

9
- mint ☐
- parsley ☐
- grass ☐
- oregano ☐
- thyme ☐

10
- chair ☐
- table ☐
- settee ☐
- sofa ☐
- bench ☐

11
- XA ☐
- VC ☐
- VE ☐
- ZB ☐

12
- HI ☐
- IN ☐
- HN ☐
- IO ☐

13
- MK ☐
- MM ☐
- MN ☐
- ML ☐

14
- LH ☐
- EG ☐
- KH ☐
- EF ☐

15
- VU ☐
- FE ☐
- HG ☐
- ED ☐

16
- MI ☐
- MO ☐
- MP ☐
- MQ ☐

17
- TP ☐
- XW ☐
- XT ☐
- TQ ☐

18
- 1 ☐
- 2 ☐
- 3 ☐
- 4 ☐
- 5 ☐

19
- Arthur ☐
- Richard ☐
- Charles ☐
- Henry ☐
- James ☐

20
- Rover ☐
- Breaks ☐
- Joey ☐
- Bristle ☐
- Max ☐

21
- RID ☐
- AID ☐
- DICE ☐
- RICE ☐
- ICED ☐

22
- CLOD ☐
- LOUD ☐
- DARE ☐
- CARE ☐
- LARE ☐

23
- WAS ☐
- SEWER ☐
- SWEAR ☐
- SPEAR ☐
- ASP ☐

24
- PAIN ☐
- PINT ☐
- SAND ☐
- SAID ☐
- PANT ☐

25
PILL ☐
SILL ☐
SAND ☐
TILL ☐
STAN ☐

26
TAR ☐
EAR ☐
ROVER ☐
TEA ☐
TOVER ☐

27
EAR ☐
WAR ☐
DEAM ☐
DAME ☐
DRAM ☐

28
0 ☐
1 ☐
2 ☐
3 ☐

29
0 ☐
1 ☐
2 ☐
3 ☐

30
0 ☐
1 ☐
2 ☐
3 ☐

31
0 ☐
1 ☐
2 ☐
3 ☐

32
TRIPE ☐
TRICE ☐
TWICE ☐
STRIP ☐

33
SHOW ☐
SLOW ☐
STOW ☐
STEW ☐

34
HEAR ☐
DEAF ☐
FEAR ☐
FACE ☐

35
SAID ☐
TAPE ☐
PAID ☐
VALE ☐

36
BEEF ☐
DEED ☐
BEAD ☐
BEET ☐

37
DEAD ☐
FEED ☐
FADE ☐
FACE ☐

38
ARROW ☐
FLEET ☐
BEECH ☐
ADDER ☐

39
COLD ☐
APED ☐
AGED ☐
CODE ☐

40
CHILL ☐
CHILD ☐
CHIDE ☐
CLASP ☐

41
JULY ☐
JANE ☐
JACK ☐
JAPE ☐

42
feet ☐
fete ☐
level ☐
fleet ☐
feel ☐
felt ☐

43
feet ☐
fete ☐
level ☐
fleet ☐
feel ☐
felt ☐

44
feet ☐
fete ☐
level ☐
fleet ☐
feel ☐
felt ☐

45
feet ☐
fete ☐
level ☐
fleet ☐
feel ☐
felt ☐

46
feet ☐
fete ☐
level ☐
fleet ☐
feel ☐
felt ☐

47
feet ☐
fete ☐
level ☐
fleet ☐
feel ☐
felt ☐

48
recite ☐
tricky ☐
lecture ☐
cities ☐
tracer ☐

49
travel ☐
latrine ☐
traitor ☐
retrace ☐
invent ☐

50
fount ☐
full ☐
bounty ☐
spider ☐
train ☐

51
gliding ☐
tight ☐
nation ☐
tonal ☐
laugh ☐

52
rested ☐
trees ☐
return ☐
retrace ☐
inspect ☐

53
moment ☐
cockle ☐
calmer ☐
voted ☐
comet ☐

54
trowel ☐
salted ☐
moult ☐
assemble ☐
mercy ☐

55
particle ☐
crate ☐
trace ☐
trail ☐
alert ☐

56
quaint ☐
quite ☐
quips ☐
quest ☐
quoit ☐

57
scintillate ☐
loser ☐
clasp ☐
close ☐
scupper ☐

58
pat ☐
go ☐
hit ☐
rat ☐
share ☐
tern ☐

59
pear ☐
post ☐
peat ☐
age ☐
arm ☐
every ☐

60
under ☐	hedge ☐
between ☐	ground ☐
on ☐	earth ☐

61
before ☐	scales ☐
every ☐	weight ☐
over ☐	height ☐

62
up ☐	sell ☐
down ☐	buy ☐
in ☐	keep ☐

63
wake ☐	even ☐
care ☐	less ☐
take ☐	more ☐

64
my ☐	man ☐
at ☐	self ☐
be ☐	person ☐

65
before ☐	soon ☐
now ☐	noon ☐
after ☐	late ☐

66
drag ☐	off ☐
pull ☐	it ☐
heave ☐	on ☐

67
pig ☐	mud ☐
horse ☐	sticky ☐
cow ☐	pat ☐

EXAMPLE
pupil ▣	student ▣
lesson ☐	desk ☐
book ☐	chalk ☐

68
small ☐	bit ☐
mouse ☐	piece ☐
big ☐	little ☐

69
quick ☐	quaint ☐
quiet ☐	fast ☐
queer ☐	slow ☐

70
stare ☐	face ☐
smile ☐	chin ☐
look ☐	grin ☐

71
go ☐	stroll ☐
run ☐	roll ☐
walk ☐	fall ☐

72
where ☐	question ☐
wonder ☐	answer ☐
wander ☐	request ☐

73
success ☐	entrance ☐
access ☐	exit ☐
excess ☐	cinema ☐

74
gentle ☐	soft ☐
justice ☐	blonde ☐
peace ☐	lore ☐

75
greasy ☐	acne ☐
spots ☐	arms ☐
bits ☐	legs ☐

76
clear ☐	nice ☐
water ☐	good ☐
seaside ☐	pure ☐

77
socks ☐	washing ☐
laundry ☐	dishes ☐
money ☐	kitchen ☐

78
| bough ☐ |
| bottle ☐ |
| battle ☐ |
| brainless ☐ |
| billowed ☐ |

79
| tracking ☐ |
| though ☐ |
| through ☐ |
| trodden ☐ |
| tickle ☐ |

80
| deaden ☐ |
| doctor ☐ |
| dreamed ☐ |
| duchess ☐ |
| delicious ☐ |

81
| marquis ☐ |
| mistress ☐ |
| monstrous ☐ |
| monastic ☐ |
| manner ☐ |

82
| nettle ☐ |
| noiseless ☐ |
| neither ☐ |
| neighbour ☐ |
| negligence ☐ |

83
| orator ☐ |
| outface ☐ |
| opened ☐ |
| oppress ☐ |
| occasion ☐ |

84
| unlace ☐ |
| useless ☐ |
| usually ☐ |
| umpire ☐ |
| urchin ☐ |

85
| closed ☐ |
| called ☐ |
| cleverly ☐ |
| compress ☐ |
| crater ☐ |

1
- a ☐
- b ☐
- c ☐
- d ☐

2
- a ☐
- b ☐
- c ☐
- d ☐

3
- a ☐
- b ☐
- c ☐
- d ☐

4
- a ☐
- b ☐
- c ☐
- d ☐

5
- a ☐
- b ☐
- c ☐
- d ☐

6
- A ☐
- B ☐
- C ☐
- D ☐

7
- A ☐
- B ☐
- C ☐
- D ☐

8
- Julie ☐
- Ken ☐
- Tom ☐
- Jerry ☐

9
- Istia ☐
- Damatia ☐
- Riskland ☐
- Grestoland ☐
- Estinia ☐

10
- Jeff ☐
- Sally ☐
- Kim ☐

11
- inquire ☐
- invest ☐
- interest ☐
- ask ☐
- tell ☐
- reveal ☐

12
- convex ☐
- perspex ☐
- perplex ☐
- game ☐
- jigsaw ☐
- puzzle ☐

13
- retrieve ☐
- rest ☐
- reprieve ☐
- carry ☐
- fetch ☐
- buy ☐

14
- fun ☐
- happiness ☐
- sadness ☐
- outside ☐
- sorrow ☐
- tears ☐

15
- mend ☐
- expensive ☐
- exchange ☐
- market ☐
- buy ☐
- transfer ☐

16
- peak ☐
- look ☐
- hear ☐
- same ☐
- summit ☐
- some ☐

17
- to ☐
- two ☐
- too ☐
- less ☐
- also ☐
- only ☐

18
- carefully ☐
- speedily ☐
- slowly ☐
- truly ☐
- gently ☐
- quickly ☐

19
- diamond ☐
- sparkle ☐
- ruby ☐
- glitter ☐
- emerald ☐
- sapphire ☐

20
- music ☐
- notes ☐
- keyboard ☐
- songs ☐
- strings ☐
- sound ☐

21
- programme ☐
- screen ☐
- sound ☐
- seats ☐
- sight ☐
- play ☐

22
- wool ☐
- needle ☐
- old ☐
- drawing ☐
- paintbrush ☐
- sketch ☐

23
- ending ☐
- theatre ☐
- sad ☐
- funny ☐
- clown ☐
- new ☐

24
- one ☐
- two ☐
- three ☐
- four ☐
- five ☐
- double ☐

25
- danger ☐
- fear ☐
- trouble ☐
- sadness ☐
- feeling ☐
- emotion ☐

26
- rain ☐
- wind ☐
- flakes ☐
- wet ☐
- stones ☐
- winter ☐

27
- trail ☐
- roar ☐
- speed ☐
- exhaust ☐
- noise ☐
- fumes ☐

28
- fry ☐
- pig ☐
- grill ☐
- sheep ☐
- farm ☐
- wool ☐

29
- carpet ☐
- floor ☐
- furry ☐
- wall ☐
- floral ☐
- stripes ☐

30
- CLUE ☐
- BLUE ☐
- CLUB ☐
- CLOG ☐

31
- MINE ☐
- PINE ☐
- FINE ☐
- MIRE ☐

32
- ZOOM ☐
- POOL ☐
- ROOM ☐
- SOON ☐

33
- SUP ☐
- SUN ☐
- SOP ☐
- ROT ☐

34
- OWE ☐
- ORB ☐
- NUB ☐
- NOD ☐

35
- NOSE ☐
- ROSE ☐
- RISE ☐
- NOTE ☐

36
- SEEK ☐
- PEEK ☐
- SEEN ☐
- SEEP ☐

37
- SUM ☐
- RIM ☐
- SUN ☐
- SIN ☐

38
- WHY ☐
- YET ☐
- WET ☐
- YES ☐

39
- franc ☐
- peseta ☐
- pasta ☐
- cent ☐
- penny ☐

40
- picnic ☐
- banquet ☐
- meal ☐
- starvation ☐
- buffet ☐

41
- soap ☐
- toothpaste ☐
- flannel ☐
- fork ☐
- bubblebath ☐

42
- carrot ☐
- pork ☐
- beef ☐
- chicken ☐
- lamb ☐

43
- grumpy ☐
- grizzle ☐
- moping ☐
- grand ☐
- moaning ☐

44
- satin ☐
- silk ☐
- cotton ☐
- wool ☐
- crimplene ☐

45
- port ☐
- wine ☐
- coffee ☐
- brandy ☐
- champagne ☐

46
- brass ☐
- gold ☐
- silver ☐
- emerald ☐
- diamond ☐

47
- plaice ☐
- pike ☐
- cod ☐
- haddock ☐
- sole ☐

48
- fantasy ☐
- pleurisy ☐
- pneumonia ☐
- bronchitis ☐
- asthma ☐

49
- pub ☐
- in ☐
- inn ☐
- quick ☐
- quest ☐
- quiet ☐

50
- for ☐
- four ☐
- flaw ☐
- tea ☐
- tiny ☐
- teen ☐

51
- bill ☐
- bob ☐
- frank ☐
- invite ☐
- incense ☐
- incur ☐

52
- child ☐
- children ☐
- school ☐
- nuts ☐
- hood ☐
- wood ☐

53
- goat ☐
- farm ☐
- kid ☐
- near ☐
- not ☐
- nap ☐

54
- clever ☐
- cope ☐
- manage ☐
- good ☐
- quiet ☐
- able ☐

55
- pair ☐
- part ☐
- past ☐
- ridge ☐
- hill ☐
- top ☐

56
- queer ☐
- quest ☐
- quiet ☐
- ion ☐
- any ☐
- on ☐

57
- how ☐
- nobody ☐
- every ☐
- which ☐
- where ☐
- what ☐

58
- Winter ☐
- Spring ☐
- Summer ☐
- Autumn ☐

59
- Carrots ☐
- Leeks ☐
- Cabbage ☐
- Sprouts ☐
- Cauliflower ☐

60
- Winter ☐
- Spring ☐
- Summer ☐
- Autumn ☐

61
- Carrots ☐
- Leeks ☐
- Cabbage ☐
- Sprouts ☐
- Cauliflower ☐

62
- Winter ☐
- Spring ☐
- Summer ☐
- Autumn ☐

63
- Winter ☐
- Spring ☐
- Summer ☐
- Autumn ☐

64
- Winter ☐
- Spring ☐
- Summer ☐
- Autumn ☐

65
- Winter ☐
- Spring ☐
- Summer ☐
- Autumn ☐

66
- Carrots ☐
- Leeks ☐
- Cabbage ☐
- Sprouts ☐
- Cauliflower ☐

67
- 0 ☐
- 1 ☐
- 2 ☐
- 3 ☐
- 4 ☐

68
- 0 ☐
- 1 ☐
- 2 ☐
- 3 ☐
- 4 ☐

69
- 0 ☐
- 1 ☐
- 2 ☐
- 3 ☐
- 4 ☐

70
- 0 ☐
- 1 ☐
- 2 ☐
- 3 ☐
- 4 ☐

71
- 0 ☐
- 1 ☐
- 2 ☐
- 3 ☐
- 4 ☐

72
- A ☐
- B ☐
- C ☐
- D ☐
- E ☐

73
- cow ☐
- horse ☐
- kangeroo ☐
- bucking ☐
- moaning ☐
- driving ☐
- colourful ☐
- crazy ☐
- windy ☐

74
- flowers ☐
- computers ☐
- records ☐
- invented ☐
- revolved ☐
- picked ☐
- fields ☐
- hotel ☐
- desk ☐

75
- pennies ☐
- pounds ☐
- cents ☐
- Japanese ☐
- Italian ☐
- American ☐
- lire ☐
- yen ☐
- dollar ☐

76
- ant ☐
- duck ☐
- buffalo ☐
- blown ☐
- run ☐
- washed ☐
- frozen ☐
- running ☐
- sticky ☐

77
- jodhpurs ☐
- skates ☐
- skis ☐
- running ☐
- riding ☐
- racing ☐
- lake ☐
- horse ☐
- windmill ☐

78
- man ☐
- judge ☐
- drunkard ☐
- alcohol ☐
- quickly ☐
- water ☐
- bench ☐
- tree ☐
- school ☐

79
- packet ☐
- postcard ☐
- pen ☐
- prism ☐
- holiday ☐
- chateau ☐
- Torquay ☐
- torment ☐
- terror ☐

80
- pepper ☐
- vinegar ☐
- salt ☐
- poison ☐
- cover ☐
- flavour ☐
- grass ☐
- potatoes ☐
- steam ☐

81

blind ☐	vibrations ☐	explore ☐
actress ☐	touch ☐	invent ☐
spiders ☐	sight ☐	destroy ☐

82

Alex ☐
Jan ☐
Ivan ☐
Rebecca ☐
Gwen ☐

83

1 ☐
2 ☐
3 ☐
4 ☐
5 ☐

84

Russian ☐
French ☐
Dutch ☐
Spanish ☐
Arabic ☐
Greek ☐

85

0 ☐
1 ☐
2 ☐
3 ☐
4 ☐

END OF PAPER 3

1

December ☐
April ☐
July ☐
September ☐

2

Osterdam ☐
Sydbourne ☐
Hudderspool ☐
Croscow ☐
Delfi ☐

3

Osterdam ☐
Hudderspool ☐
Croscow ☐
Delfi ☐

4

December ☐
April ☐
July ☐
September ☐

5

Osterdam ☐
Sydbourne ☐
Hudderspool ☐
Croscow ☐
Delfi ☐

6

0 ☐
1 ☐
2 ☐
3 ☐
4 ☐

7

December ☐
April ☐
July ☐
September ☐

8

December ☐
April ☐
July ☐
September ☐

9

Osterdam ☐
Sydbourne ☐
Hudderspool ☐
Croscow ☐
Delfi ☐

10

Osterdam ☐
Sydbourne ☐
Hudderspool ☐
Croscow ☐
Delfi ☐

11

listen ☐
dream ☐
hear ☐
watch ☐
concentrate ☐

12

justice ☐
peace ☐
government ☐
equality ☐
truth ☐

13

river ☐
stream ☐
estuary ☐
tributary ☐
island ☐

14

fall ☐
mountain ☐
glacier ☐
summit ☐
rock ☐

15

book ☐
magazine ☐
television ☐
leaflet ☐
booklet ☐

16

wood ☐
paper ☐
coal ☐
plastic ☐
peat ☐

17

star ☐
meteor ☐
astronaut ☐
comet ☐
planet ☐

18

necklace ☐
gold ☐
silver ☐
platinum ☐
steel ☐

19

B ☐
T ☐
W ☐
S ☐

20

T ☐
H ☐
Y ☐
S ☐

21

D ☐
E ☐
Y ☐
T ☐

22
- O ☐
- A ☐
- Y ☐
- E ☐

23
- H ☐
- E ☐
- T ☐
- M ☐

24
- K ☐
- H ☐
- T ☐
- R ☐

25
- T ☐
- S ☐
- E ☐
- B ☐

26
- S ☐
- T ☐
- Y ☐
- D ☐

27
- N ☐
- S ☐
- T ☐
- K ☐

28
- Q ☐
- P ☐
- O ☐
- K ☐
- L ☐

29
- G ☐
- F ☐
- H ☐
- K ☐
- J ☐

30
- S ☐
- W ☐
- V ☐
- U ☐
- T ☐

31
- K ☐
- M ☐
- L ☐
- O ☐
- J ☐

32
- 10 ☐
- 11 ☐
- 12 ☐
- 13 ☐
- 14 ☐

33
- 2 ☐
- 4 ☐
- 0 ☐
- 1 ☐
- 10 ☐

34
- 50 ☐
- 65 ☐
- 40 ☐
- 25 ☐
- 20 ☐

35
- 18 ☐
- 15 ☐
- 21 ☐
- 12 ☐
- 24 ☐

36
- 15 ☐
- 10 ☐
- 18 ☐
- 11 ☐
- 12 ☐

37
- 19 ☐
- 18 ☐
- 20 ☐
- 22 ☐
- 21 ☐

38
- 24 ☐
- 32 ☐
- 16 ☐
- 48 ☐
- 52 ☐

39
- anchor ☐
- ranch ☐
- bleach ☐
- manage ☐
- mangy ☐

40
- hinted ☐
- shine ☐
- thane ☐
- later ☐
- night ☐

41
- rickety ☐
- character ☐
- traitor ☐
- creature ☐
- cured ☐

42
- failing ☐
- feeling ☐
- gloried ☐
- carafe ☐
- glorious ☐

43
- dearest ☐
- slowly ☐
- wronged ☐
- drowsy ☐
- grouse ☐

44
- phonic ☐
- loop ☐
- lonely ☐
- helped ☐
- honed ☐

45
- horse ☐
- rattle ☐
- whine ☐
- bother ☐
- white ☐

46
- rough ☐
- ferry ☐
- trifle ☐
- every ☐
- fierce ☐

47
- tractor ☐
- strait ☐
- truth ☐
- rupture ☐
- state ☐

48
- their ☐
- thread ☐
- wrath ☐
- trees ☐
- drape ☐

49
- a ☐
- b ☐
- c ☐
- d ☐

50
- a ☐
- b ☐
- c ☐
- d ☐

51
- 0 ☐
- 1 ☐
- 2 ☐
- 3 ☐

52
- 0 ☐
- 1 ☐
- 2 ☐
- 3 ☐

53
- 0 ☐
- 1 ☐
- 2 ☐
- 3 ☐

54
- 0 ☐
- 1 ☐
- 2 ☐
- 3 ☐

55
- Tom ☐
- Dick ☐
- Harriet ☐
- Elsa ☐

56
- Richard ☐
- James ☐
- Robert ☐
- Joan ☐
- Gillian ☐
- Jessica ☐

57
- toes ☐
- squeeze ☐
- foot ☐
- dance ☐
- pound ☐
- money ☐

58
- name ☐
- flower ☐
- grow ☐
- tree ☐
- garden ☐
- path ☐

59
- one ☐
- none ☐
- gone ☐
- some ☐
- to ☐
- two ☐

60
- trap ☐
- catched ☐
- caught ☐
- brought ☐
- shop ☐
- bought ☐

61
- pale ☐
- people ☐
- human ☐
- animal ☐
- coat ☐
- hairy ☐

62
- window ☐
- break ☐
- clear ☐
- hard ☐
- door ☐
- brown ☐

63
- Jenny ☐
- kind ☐
- smile ☐
- gun ☐
- mean ☐
- war ☐

64
- buy ☐
- wear ☐
- head ☐
- hand ☐
- warm ☐
- leather ☐

65
- one ☐
- switch ☐
- off ☐
- out ☐
- put ☐
- go ☐

66
- leather ☐
- heels ☐
- winter ☐
- slim ☐
- summer ☐
- thin ☐

67
- fairness ☐
- courts ☐
- lawyers ☐
- statue ☐
- love ☐
- freedom ☐

68
- foolish ☐
- clever ☐
- wise ☐
- silly ☐
- steady ☐
- numb ☐

69
- weird ☐
- bad ☐
- sad ☐
- right ☐
- good ☐
- rotten ☐

70
- politician ☐
- Labour ☐
- Tory ☐
- govern ☐
- statesman ☐
- justice ☐

71
- fight ☐
- trite ☐
- three ☐
- stale ☐
- bread ☐
- air ☐

72
- sage ☐
- wage ☐
- rage ☐
- fury ☐
- worry ☐
- sorry ☐

73
- eating ☐
- drinking ☐
- food ☐
- question ☐
- hunger ☐
- chewing ☐

74
- report ☐
- support ☐
- deport ☐
- detain ☐
- sustain ☐
- refrain ☐

75
- handle ☐
- bangle ☐
- reveal ☐
- hold ☐
- gold ☐
- resolve ☐

76
- new ☐
- history ☐
- old ☐
- gold ☐
- antique ☐
- shop ☐

77
- new ☐
- yesterday ☐
- tomorrow ☐
- news ☐
- recent ☐
- modern ☐

78
- MISS ☐
- MOSS ☐
- MESS ☐
- MASS ☐

79
- MOOT ☐
- MEET ☐
- MOON ☐
- SOON ☐

80
- SING ☐
- SONG ☐
- SEAT ☐
- SEAM ☐

81
- NEAT ☐
- NAME ☐
- TIME ☐
- TAME ☐

82
- SAME ☐
- SEAT ☐
- STEM ☐
- STAG ☐

83
- REST ☐
- NEST ☐
- TEAM ☐
- NEAT ☐

84
- MEAN ☐
- SAME ☐
- MEAT ☐
- SEAM ☐

85
- SING ☐
- SONG ☐
- RING ☐
- SANE ☐

PAPER 1

1.	MEET	22.	green	43.	heavily	64.	ROUT
2.	IN	23.	blue	44.	relegate	65.	PORK
3.	THE	24.	black	45.	predator	66.	catapult
4.	OLD	25.	France	46.	anorak	67.	ice-cream
5.	BARN	26.	crayon	47.	sorrowful	68.	glass
6.	AT	27.	bus	48.	poultice	69.	necklace
7.	MIDNIGHT	28.	mammal	49.	licence	70.	wood
8.	WITH	29.	wall	50.	C	71.	Britain
9.	YOUR	30.	Jason	51.	D	72.	apple
10.	TORCH	31.	L, O	52.	B	73.	fish
11.	COLT	32.	S, Q	53.	E	74.	bush
12.	MEET	33.	O, U	54.	A	75.	boat
13.	HIDE	34.	F, X	55.	E	76.	eight/four
14.	CAD	35.	O, C	56.	A	77.	sheep/worm
15.	GAVE	36.	K, L	57.	C	78.	watch/listen
16.	DICE	37.	M, P	58.	ROOT	79.	cat/duck
17.	FACE	38.	M, N	59.	COOT	80.	reptile/mammal
18.	ROSE	39.	U, Z	60.	PROP	81.	bricks/ice
19.	KISS	40.	wearily	61.	TRUCK	82.	rails/road
20.	CAGE	41.	jumper	62.	TROUT	83.	horse/cow
21.	red	42.	retrace	63.	CURT	84.	pig/sheep
						85.	ears/tongue

PAPER 2

1.	music	22.	LOUD/CARE	43.	LEVEL	64.	myself
2.	garage	23.	ASP/SEWER	44.	FEEL	65.	afternoon
3.	tale	24.	PANT/SAID	45.	FEET	66.	dragon
4.	Moon	25.	SAND/TILL	46.	FLEET	67.	cowpat
5.	black	26.	TEA/ROVER	47.	FETE	68.	small/little
6.	London	27.	WAR/DAME	48.	recite	69.	quick/fast
7.	swallow	28.	1	49.	latrine	70.	smile/grin
8.	view	29.	2	50.	fount	71.	walk/stroll
9.	grass	30.	3	51.	tonal	72.	wonder/question
10.	table	31.	0	52.	trees	73.	access/entrance
11.	VE	32.	TWICE	53.	comet	74.	gentle/soft
12.	IN	33.	SLOW	54.	moult	75.	spots/acne
13.	MK	34.	DEAF	55.	trail	76.	clear/pure
14.	KH	35.	TAPE	56.	quoit	77.	laundry/washing
15.	FE	36.	BEEF	57.	close	78.	bough
16.	MQ	37.	FACE	58.	pattern	79.	tracking
17.	TP	38.	BEECH	59.	postage	80.	dreamed
18.	2	39.	AGED	60.	underground	81.	monastic
19.	Richard	40.	CHIDE	61.	overweight	82.	nettle
20.	Breaks	41.	JANE	62.	upkeep	83.	orator
21.	AID/RICE	42.	FELT	63.	careless	84.	useless
						85.	compress

PAPER 3

1. c	22. needle/paintbrush	43. grand	64. Autumn
2. d	23. sad/funny	44. crimplene	65. Summer
3. c	24. two/four	45. coffee	66. carrots
4. b	25. fear/sadness	46. brass	67. 3
5. c	26. flakes/stones	47. pike	68. 3
6. A	27. trail/exhaust	48. fantasy	69. 0
7. D	28. pig/sheep	49. inquest	70. 0
8. Ken	29. floor/wall	50. fourteen	71. 2
9. Damatia	30. BLUE	51. frankincense	72. A
10. Jeff	31. MINE	52. childhood	73. horse/bucking/windy
11. inquire/ask	32. ROOM	53. kidnap	74. flowers/picked/fields
12. perplex/puzzle	33. SUN	54. manageable	75. cents/American/dollar
13. retrieve/fetch	34. ORB	55. partridge	76. ant/washed/running
14. sadness/sorrow	35. NOSE	56. question	77. jodhpurs/riding/horse
15. exchange/transfer	36. SEEK	57. everywhere	78. drunkard/alcohol/bench
16. peak/summit	37. RIM	58. Summer	79. postcard/holiday/Torquay
17. too/also	38. WET	59. cabbage	80. salt/flavour/potatoes
18. speedily/quickly	39. pasta	60. Summer	81. blind/touch/explore
19. sparkle/glitter	40. starvation	61. cauliflower	82. Jan
20. keyboard/strings	41. fork	62. Winter	83. 3
21. sound/sight	42. carrot	63. Autumn	84. Russian
			85. 2

PAPER 4

1. July	22. O	43. grouse	64. head/hand
2. Croscow	23. H	44. loop	65. off/out
3. Delfi	24. T	45. bother	66. winter/summer
4. December	25. B	46. fierce	67. fairness/freedom
5. Croscow	26. D	47. state	68. foolish/silly
6. 4	27. K	48. thread	69. bad/rotten
7. July	28. P, K	49. c	70. politician/statesman
8. July	29. G, J	50. c	71. trite/stale
9. Sydbourne	30. U, W	51. 3	72. rage/fury
10. Hudderspool	31. L, J	52. 1	73. eating/chewing
11. dream	32. 10, 13	53. 2	74. support/sustain
12. government	33. 10, 0	54. 0	75. handle/hold
13. island	34. 50, 25	55. Dick	76. old/antique
14. fall	35. 15, 21	56. Robert/Gillian	77. new/modern
15. television	36. 11, 15	57. foot/pound	78. MESS
16. plastic	37. 21, 18	58. flower/tree	79. MOOT
17. astronaut	38. 16, 32	59. one/two	80. SONG
18. necklace	39. manage	60. caught/bought	81. TIME
19. W	40. thane	61. human/animal	82. STAG
20. S	41. cured	62. window/door	83. NEST
21. D	42. failing	63. kind/mean	84. SEAM
			85. SING